EQ and You

Understand, apply, and enhance your emotional intelligence.

Real life application and transformation
Self | Love | Happiness | Career | Conflict

© 2016 by Lena Cohen

All rights reserved.

Cover Work:

Graphics/Production By: Gary Robinson of LogoGlo

Table of Contents

Introduction

Chapter 1   1
Understanding EQ

Chapter 2   7
EQ and You

Chapter 4   17
EQ and Love

Chapter 5   27
EQ and Life Happiness

Chapter 6   36
EQ and Your Career

Chapter 7   49
EQ and Conflict

Introduction

It's interesting; the way we view and interpret emotions. The way we categorize them, how we're taught to hide or ignore them, and how we determine who's "allowed" to have or show them and when. It's all quite fascinating when you really look at it. What's even more interesting is that we're usually way into our adulthood before we really learn how to identify, categorize, and manage our emotions properly—in a way that is healthy, positive, and beneficial.

Emotions are such a huge part of our everyday lives. They dictate so much of what exists and doesn't exist in our world, from the tangible to the intangible. Emotions, and our ability or inability to manage them, determines everything. They impact how we operate, the way we treat people, how we process information, our perception and reception of others and ultimately how far we go in life. Having a heightened sense of emotional intelligence is the key for success, in so many areas of our lives.

So often we're just moving through life; not assessing ourselves or our emotions. My intention with this handbook is to help you understand, apply, and enhance your emotional intelligence in a way that creates a shift in your world and success in your endeavors. This book will guide you step by step in some of the most important areas of your life, helping you reflect on how you manage your emotions, and creating a more self-aware existence.

Chapter 1
Understanding EQ

First things first let's define emotional intelligence so we're all on the same page. I want to share several definitions with you, as I believe they all embody different aspects of emotional intelligence that are important.

"Emotional intelligence is your ability to recognize and understand emotions in yourself and others, and your ability to use this awareness to manage your behavior and relationship."
-Dr. Travis Bradberry and Jean Greaves

"Emotional intelligence (EQ) is the ability to identify, use, understand, and manage emotions in positive ways to relieve stress, communicate effectively, empathize with others, overcome challenges, and defuse conflict… The ability to monitor one's own and others' feelings, to discriminate among them, and to use this information to guide one's thinking and action."

"Emotional intelligence involves the ability to perceive accurately, appraise, and express emotion; the ability to access and/or generate feelings when
they facilitate thought; the ability to understand emotion and emotional knowledge; and the ability to regulate emotions to promote emotional and intellectual growth."
-Salovey and Mayer

Of course, as studies grow and more people become familiar with this fairly new concept, various definitions can be found. However, these shine the brightest for me because they encompass many of the things I teach on a daily basis.

Now that you have a clear definition of what emotional intelligence is; I'm going to introduce you to the core principles that determine whether or not you have a high EQ. They are the foundational elements that will help you refine, develop, apply, and/or enhance your emotional intelligence. After examining each principle we'll go on to explore how each of these elements can impact various areas of your life.

1. Self-awareness

Self-awareness is most often seen at the top of the list or identified as the first step when discussing EQ. I personally believe it is the cornerstone of emotional intelligence, without it out everything else falls through. Self-awareness is the ability to consciously identify and acknowledge one's own feelings, motives, and desires. It's having a clear perception and understanding of who you are and why you do the things you do. Self-awareness is focusing on yourself, in order to evaluate and compare your current behaviors to your internal standards and values.

It's all about gaining a better understanding of yourself and your emotions—getting to the core of who you really are. This concept is a fundamental tool and must be developed first so that you can successfully move on to the other principles. Self-awareness is all about knowing how to identify and operate in your strengths and growth areas. It's having a strong understanding of who you are and what you represent and/or stand for. Knowing yourself first, is the key to successfully enhancing your emotional intelligence and using it in a way that separates you from others.

2. Self - Management / Control

Once you've learned how to identify "who you are," by recognizing your emotions, motives, and desires; it's imperative that you learn how to manage them properly. This is an element I'm sure we all fall short of sometimes. However, when we are more self-aware and remain in a present state of consciousness, we are more likely to take our time and acknowledge the thought, idea, action or emotion and respond accordingly. This is a principle that some find difficult and must be practiced on a daily basis for success.

Self-control is how effectively you're able to manage and align your emotions with your values and/or standard of living. That's why it's important to develop a strong sense of self-awareness first, because you have to know what those core standards, morals, and values are in order to manage your emotions effectively. You can't begin to practice self-control if you don't know where your limits and values are. Self-awareness may be who you are, but self-control is about who you want to be. It's about having the ability to slow down, stop, and adjust your feelings in a way that puts you in line with the person you desire to be.

3. Empathy

Understanding your own emotions can be hard enough, and trying to understand someone else's can be even more difficult. Making a strong effort to understand

and interpret someone else's emotions can be extremely taxing at times. There are several factors that make people see and feel things differently. You never really know what's going on inside someone else's mind or heart. However, you don't always have to know exactly what's going on with a person to connect with them, that's where empathy and compassion comes in.

Empathy is simply being able to recognize what's going on in someone else's life. It's attempting to understand how they feel, what emotions they may be going through, and being considerate with your response to them. It's acknowledging the person and being able to put yourself in their place. It may not always be easy, but empathy is a social responsibility, and it helps you develop a sense of social awareness for how you treat and respond to others.

How you interact with people is critical to the next and last principle, which is building relationships. If you can't begin to identify with and/or recognize the needs of others, you run the risk of damaging relationships. Those who struggle with the ability to empathize are often known to be cold and difficult to bond with. They struggle with being empathetic for many reasons, but when they let down their walls the next principle has the opportunity to flourish.

4. Relationship Building / Social Awareness

As you can see, all of these principles are interconnected in a way in which each one requires you to excel in the other. In order for you to build, manage, and positively impact relationships the above principles must be put into practice. Social awareness isn't about being friendly or whether you like someone or not. It's about having human decency and respect for others, treating people the way you'd like to be treated.

Do you ever stop to think about how you talk to people, or how you respond them? Are you aware of the tone in which you speak to others? When you address people, are you conscious of your body language? Is it appropriate? Do you use active listening skills when people are conveying their message? Are you a person who can agree to disagree, so all parties can come to a resolution? Do you allow your peers to express their thoughts and opinions freely? Do you insist on being right all the time?

These things matter when you're trying to develop and/or build stronger, healthier relationships. It's a pertinent part of improving your emotional intelligence. Your level of social awareness often helps people determine whether or not they want to continue to be in a relationship with you, work with you, and/or be associated with you at all. The fact is, we aren't here alone, and how we interact with others matters.

I hope you have a better understanding of what emotional intelligence is and how beneficial it can be to your everyday life. Although these are in depths concepts that require time, energy, focus, and consistency—I wanted to provide a simple concise body of work that would allow you to receive the information in a way that wasn't so daunting. Change, in any department of our lives, can be challenging. Especially with things like, learning how to tell yourself and others the truth about how you feel, controlling strong passionate emotions like anger and betrayal, and managing close personal relationships. It's all a learning process and takes time.

Now that you have a better understanding, we can move on to application (ways to implement EQ), enhancement (ways to go above and beyond for continued development), and reflection (an opportunity for you to see yourself clearly). With these tools you'll be able to develop and/or refine your emotional intelligence in no time.

Chapter 2
EQ and You

You are the central focal point of your life. Everything you say, every action you take, all that you are, and the decisions you make, all derive from a single thought, emotion, and/or feeling. This is why developing your emotional intelligence is so important. If you're not paying attention and categorizing your emotions appropriately, than who or what is? Think about it. Are you allowing outside people, places, and things to control your emotions—ultimately, controlling you and your life?

Our emotions can only be categorized one of two ways—positive or negative. The emotion either feels good and we encourage it or it makes us uncomfortable and provides us with a level of dis-ease. Developing a high EQ requires you to do your best at identifying and redirecting negative emotions. Now, let me be clear and elaborate. No one expects you to redirect a strong negative emotion like anger to a strong positive emotion like joy. However, the goal may be to get from angry to annoyed or irritated. This way you can better manage the situation and its outcomes.

That's what this entire book is about; you being in control and able to obtain more positive outcomes in your life and with others. People don't realize the power emotions have in their lives. Each and every day an emotion is driving your actions, and it's up to you to monitor and manage those emotions closely. Each emotion leads to an action, and those actions lead to habits which ultimately leads to a way of life. You have to ask yourself, what type of life am I leading? Am I proud of my actions? Am I content with the relationships I have in my life? What am I doing to improve my overall sense of well-being?

The following pages (at the end of each section) are for you to fill in. When you want to get to know someone, you ask them questions. Here, you're going to ask yourself questions and get to know who you really are. These questions are meant to be a deep dive, giving you the introspective awareness you need to improve your EQ.

Applying Emotional Intelligence
Self-Awareness

- Who are you?
Learn how to open up and be honest with yourself first.

_____
_____

- What qualities/characteristics do you possess?
Begin to identify and acknowledge the real you.

_____
_____

- Do these traits directly correlate with your morals, values, and standards of life? Yes, or No?
Know the parameters of your ethical life limits.

- What or who defines your morals/values? Why?
Understand where/how you developed these ideals.

_____
_____

- Where can you be more honest with yourself?
This development is for you, so do your best to be real.

_____
_____

- Are you able to quickly identify and articulate what you're feeling? List emotions you consistently run from.
Think about it, do you recognize it or hide it?

_____
_____

Self-Control

- I don't think before I speak when...
Words are so powerful, be mindful of how you use them.

_____
_____

- I don't think before I act in situations where...
Understand that some actions can't be undone.

_____
_____

- I'm regretful about the consequences that came with...
Think about a time where you lost control. Was it worth it?

_____
_____

- I blow up/lose control when… I'm feeling...
Listen, to understand, before responding with emotion.

_____
_____

- Do you respond while in the emotion? Yes, or no?
Have a cool down method. Know when to remove yourself, take a deep breath, and return to the conversation or situation.

- Are you able to regroup quickly?
After a bad experience, have the ability to let it go in a timely manner. Don't harbor on it for days.

_____
_____

Empathy

- I can be judgmental when it comes to...

Learn to free yourself from judgement, it's not a good trait.

_____

_____

- People get on my nerves when they...

Why are you bothered by what other people do?

_____

_____

- How do you treat the people you dislike?

Reflect on your morals/values here.

_____

_____

- Do you ALWAYS put your wants and needs first? Yes, or no?

If so, you may want to re-evaluate your intentions.

- Can you agree to disagree? What are you trying to prove and to whom?

Learn to pick your battles. The scars may last long.

_____

_____

- Are you able to shift your energy when you're around someone you don't like or understand?

People can feel your energy before you speak or act.

_____

_____

Building Relationships

- What makes you a good person to know/associate with?
Remember relationship should be reciprocal.

_____
_____

- What emotions are you currently dealing/battling with?
Sometimes it's us, not them. Sometimes we're projecting.

_____
_____

- Where can you show more appreciation and gratitude?
Are you currently taking someone for granted?

_____
_____

- Is there something you can do to build the relationship?
Sometimes the solution is easier than it seems. Let go of any pride stalling the relationship.

_____
_____

- Did you all discuss the needs of the relationship?
Communication is key.

_____
_____

- Can you learn new ways to trust the person?
If there's no trust there's no progression.

_____
_____

Enhancing Your Emotional Intelligence
Self-Awareness

- Who do you want to be?
Take it a step further, begin to think about development.

_____
_____

- What qualities/characteristics do you want to possess?
Knowing this is key to that development.

_____
_____

- Do your current morals/values reflect the person you want to be? Yes, or no?
Be prepared to face/drop any false narratives in your life.

- If the traits you possess don't correlate with your morals/values, are you prepared to create change? How?
Actions always speak louder than words!

_____
_____

- Where can I be more honest? More accountable?
You can't fix a problem you don't believe you have.

_____
_____

- Practice walking yourself through various emotions. It will help you articulate what and how you're feeling more often, in a more productive way.
Talking to yourself is perfectly okay!

Self-Control

- Always ask yourself "What are my intentions?"
Take a beat to consider your emotions and the situation.

___

- Are your actions showing love, kindness, and compassion?
Learn how to walk in the light, with grace and honor.

___

- Will you regret this action/statement?
Pause, and think about the bigger/overall picture.

___

- Are you in the right state of mind?
Things like hunger, sleep deprivation, and residual emotions, can effect your reactions.

___

- I feel like I'm losing control when...
Know where your limits are.

___

- Don't be afraid to acknowledge you faults and take responsibility for your actions.
This is where growth lives. People respect accountability.

Empathy

- Are there ways you can be more understanding?
Think about a time in your life where you could have used more empathy with someone.

_____

_____

- Who can you be more patient with?
Here is where self-control is exercised.

_____

_____

- Are you able to show respect to people you don't like?
Achieving this makes life's much easier and less stressful.

_____

_____

- What can you do for someone else today?
Take the time to encourage and/or support someone else in a way that you'd like to be supported.

_____

_____

- Can you regulate your emotions during a conversation?
Having a debate is fine, don't start a war.

_____

_____

- Are you able to put your thoughts, views, and opinions aside to hear someone else's? Yes, or no?

Building Relationships

- What characteristics make you difficult to deal with?
This requires real honesty, truth, and accountability.

_____
_____

- What emotions do you need to shift, change, or let go of for your relationships to work?
Begin to identify areas where you need healing.

_____
_____

- What kind gesture could you offer, to enhance the relationship?
Sometimes all it takes is a step in the right direction to show someone you care.

_____
_____

- Do you operate from a genuine place with this person?
Are you even capable? Is there wall up, something hindering you from this level progress? If so, what is it?

_____
_____

- Can I accurately identify what my part is in building the relationship? Yes, or No?
If not, don't be afraid to ask the other person what they need for the relationship to work.

Chapter 3
EQ and Love

Love is such a beautiful thing. It's something we crave as humans. It has the potential to heal, elevate, and open us up in ways we never thought possible. However, love requires so much of us as individuals. There's so much we have to give in order for our love to remain strong, work, and stand the test of time. It can be complicated and complex at times—because we're all so different. People see love in so many different ways. It has so many perspectives due to people's upbringing, culture, society, religion, and environment. Emotional intelligence allows us to bring those perspectives together and operate on one level playing field.

We all give and receive love in various forms, but I believe there's a few things we can all identify with that exemplify love. Things like admiration, respect, kindness, compassion, support, romance, and intimacy. Those things, you know, the "lovey-dovey" stuff—is always easily identifiable and generally sets the standard. It's the open and honest communication, forgiveness, willingness to work-it-out, empathy, and emotional support that we don't talk about as often. Probably because it scares the crap out of most people because that's where all the work is. That's where self-awareness, self-control, empathy, and relationship building are needed the most.

Although it can be scary, it doesn't have to be. Individuals that understand and display a strong sense of emotional intelligence often handle stress and difficulty in a different way. Phrases like, "We should to talk" become a beacon of light, clarity, and mutual understanding instead of something to dread or fear. It's where, "Why didn't you read the instructions?" turns into "Thank you for assembling that for me." So let's go on to explore how we can apply and enhance our emotional intelligence through love.

In the next set of questions I'm going to use the term "partner," representing a romantic relationship. However, these questions can also apply to anyone you love in your inner circle. Sometimes loving relationships with our children, friends, and/or family members need to be strengthened in order for us to be effective and succeed in our endeavors.

Applying EQ to Love
Self-Awareness

- Who are you outside of your relationship?
Healthy independence is important to self.

_____

_____

- Where can you be more expressive with your partner?
Nobody's a mind reader, be specific with your desires.

_____

_____

- My triggers are...
Know your triggers and convey them to your partner.

_____

_____

- I am still healing/hurting/upset about...
Is a past situation/incident hindering the future?

_____

_____

- What can you let slide/let go off?
Life is short, choose your arguments wisely. Recognize when they're about frivolous things.

_____

_____

- Are you able to stand strong, rebuild, and move on?
It's okay to be resilient and fight for your relationship. However, know your limits— and don't live in pain.

Self-Control

- What does a disagreement typically look like for you?
Create the standard for what respectful disagreements look like, to maintain control.

_____
_____

- What are your deepest fears/aspirations for this relationship?
This is something that should be discussed with your partner.

_____
_____

- Do you all take enough time for yourselves separately?
Relaxation and time apart, takes the intense pressure off.

_____
_____

- List ways you can change your words or delivery?
Use compassion when talking to the ones you love.

_____
_____

- Are you a, "I'm always right! My way is always better!" person?
Be willing to compromise and work towards a common positive outcome.

_____
_____

Empathy

- How do you all connect? How much time is spent together?

Make time for one another, so you can relate more.

_____

_____

- How often do you provide your undivided attention?

Technology and devices can create distance; make sure you have some one-on-one time without distractions.

_____

_____

- How often do you all misunderstand each other? Where does the breakdown in communication happen?

Show interest by listening with care, respect, and attention.

_____

_____

- When was the last time you advocated for your partner?

Show your partner you care and understand by standing by them and supporting them in their time of need.

_____

_____

- Were could you be more patient with your partner?

Allow your partner room to grow. No one is perfect. If they're working towards greatness encourage that.

_____

_____

Building Relationships

- What are your ideals about expectations in a relationship?

Make sure you're not holding your partner accountable to unrealistic expectation.

_____
_____

- Where do you all need to strengthen your relationship?

Identify growth areas and how you plan to get there.

_____
_____

- I am still carrying old baggage from...

Don't make your partner suffer the mistakes of others.

_____
_____

- Do you all spend time in meditation and/or prayer together? Yes, or no?

Having restorative refuge, time for self reflection, and being on the same page spiritually can improve the health of the relationship—it makes each person better, and able to cope with life's difficulties more effectively

- What are you really fighting about/for?

Always deal with the root of the issue. Attack it head on. You can't heal what you don't reveal.

_____
_____

Enhancing EQ with Love
Self-Awareness

- Are you fulfilling your hopes, dreams, and aspirations?
Relationships work best when both parties are happy within themselves and working towards success.

_____
_____

- What are your goals? Separate and together.
Both parties should strive to be on the same page about their future looks like?

_____
_____

- Is your tone too harsh, do you fight to kill in arguments?
Ask yourself... Is it kind? Is it true? Is it <u>necessary</u>?

_____
_____

- Where could you all use more balance?
Work together! Both parties should be putting in the effort.

_____
_____

- How can you provide more emotional support?
It's the little things that make the biggest impact

_____
_____

- Do you share the same ideals/moral beliefs? If not, is it hindering your growth. Yes, or no?

Self-Control

- Where do you need to develop as an individual?

Do you have a temper? Do you lash out? Are you mean?

_____

_____

- When was the last time you "went too far" during a conflict?

Being the bigger person gets easier the more you try

_____

_____

- Do you acknowledge when you've gone too far?

Get more comfortable with checking yourself, before your partner has to.

_____

_____

- When was the last time you asked about your partners feelings?

Use your sense of empathy to create a level of understanding.

_____

_____

- What does your daily practice look like?

Mediation, affirmations, and mantra are excellent tools for self-control.

_____

_____

Empathy

- Do you generally probe for clarity and understanding when you know something's wrong? Or leave it alone?

Ask questions, be observant, don't turn a blind eye to unusual behavior.

_____

_____

- How can you do a better job of conveying a message of solidarity when things are rough?

Sometime your partner just needs to know that you're there from them.

_____

_____

- Where could you be more willing to forgive?

Relationships don't always "work," but with resilience they can last and be restored.

_____

_____

- Do you and your partner still have room to grow? If so, in what areas?

Allow your relationship an opportunity to grow.

_____

_____

- I needed empathy when….

Think about a time you wish you had more empathy

_____

_____

Building Relationships

- Are you comfortable in your own skin?

Learn to lift each other up and embrace all the good things about each other.

_____

_____

- What makes your partner happy? Do you celebrate them when you have the opportunity?

Invest in one another, seek to understand and then execute.

_____

_____

- When you're mad, can you still see why you love them?

In the darkness choose light.

_____

_____

- Do you all have a life plan? Together and separately?

Make sure you discuss life plans (children, finances, careers, etc.) so you're both building towards the same thing.

_____

_____

- What do you expect of yourself, when it comes to the relationship? Do you have standards for yourself?

We get what we give. Sometimes we focus too much on what we want and not enough on what we can give.

_____

_____

Chapter 5
EQ and Happiness

Happiness can only derive from one place, and that's from within. When we rely on people, places, and things to make us happy, at some point we always find ourselves disappointed. Happiness is a choice, that we must choose to make every day—and it begins with us. We can choose at any time to live in optimism and positivity. A part of emotional intelligence is learning how to redirect negative energy and emotions, to more favorable ones, so you can exhibit more favorable behaviors and obtain more favorable outcomes.

When you enhance your emotional intelligence you can find happiness in things you may not have found happiness in before. You can find peace in situation that were once stressful. You can find joy and gratitude in the small wins. Having the capacity to redirect your emotions and choose happiness is a technique that can drastically change your life for the better.

People that have a high EQ know how to categorize and align their emotions properly in order to remain more in control of their lives. They don't take offense to things that don't pertain to them, because they are confident in who they are. They don't allow the thoughts and/or opinions of others to negatively effect their spirit because they're secure and have a heightened sense of self awareness. Looking forward think about all the ways you can create more happiness in your world. Think about each scenario where you can take the high road. Think about new ways of rearranging your perspective to align with your morals/values.

Applying EQ to Life Happiness
Self-Awareness

- What do you love about yourself?

Each day spend more time highlighting the things you love about yourself.

_____
_____

- What qualities might you need to change?

What habits do you need to change to live a happier life?

_____
_____

- Who or what contributes to your happiness?

It's okay for something or someone to add to your happiness, as long as it doesn't define your happiness.

_____
_____

- When I'm having a bad day I...

Develop a strategy plan to combat cloudy days.

_____
_____

- What are you most grateful for?

Focus on developing a strong sense of gratitude. When you do this your frustrations about the little things will subside.

_____
_____

Self-Control

- What are you doing to achieve your goals?

Remaining focused and having control helps you move toward the things that make you happy.

_____

_____

- What are some things you should stop doing to improve your overall health?

Health is a huge part of happiness. Yet sometimes we don't take control over the things necessary to maintain it.

_____

_____

- Who is capable of pushing your buttons?

Learn how to be proactive when it comes to interacting with people that may bring out the worst in you.

_____

_____

- Where can you be more disciplined in life?

Discipline helps you to develop more controlled behavior. You'll be less likely to go off course if you're disciplined in your behavior.

_____

_____

- I would be much happier if I stopped/started…

Again self-awareness is key.

_____

_____

Empathy

- What organization can you contribute to that would bring you joy?

What cause can you contribute to that would give you more fulfillment. How can you be of service?

_____
_____

- Who can you be less judgmental with?

Some relationships would be ten times better if we stop judging and started accepting.

_____
_____

- Where, or with whom, can you show more compassion?

We take it for granted, but things like love, compassion, and kindness fill us with happiness.

_____
_____

- How can you share your life experiences to help someone else?

Impact and legacy often brings about joy. Be someone that people can relate to, share experiences with and learn from.

_____
_____

Building Relationships

- Where can healing take place?

Are there important relationships in your life that need mending?

_____
_____

- Do you need to create boundaries with anyone in your life?

Sometimes boundaries are necessary for you to maintain your happiness.

_____
_____

- What type of people do you want/need in your life? What characteristics do you want them to possess?

Who you surround yourself with has a great impact on your daily life and mood.

_____
_____

- Do the people in your immediate circle support your dreams?

Our dreams and aspiration can be crushed if we don't have the right people in our corner.

_____
_____

Enhancing EQ to achieve Happiness
Self-Awareness

- What affirmations can you develop to achieve a better sense of self-worth, confidence and motivation?

Affirmations are a great way to develop and enhance self-love, which helps create a better sense of self-awareness.

_____
_____

- Are you afraid of change? If, so why? If not, are you operating with the intent on being happy?

Sometimes we can be afraid of losing our "old-self" and truly stepping into the new. Start changing small things and work your way up.

_____
_____

- What types of things dictate your happiness? Do they serve you in positive way?

Evaluate the "things" that bring you happiness and begin to edit anything that isn't positively beneficial.

_____
_____

- Do you take enough time for yourself?

The greatest awareness comes when we look within. Are you meditating? Are you praying? Do you take enough restoration time for your mind, body, and spirit?

_____
_____

Self-Control

- When was the last time you created a vision board or goal chart?

Having these tools often helps us stay inspired and on track towards the things that bring us fulfillment and joy.

_____
_____

- What can I do to improve my mental, physical, and emotional wellbeing?

Happiness generally comes from a holistic place. You have to take control over situations and habits that impact your overall health. Be proactive!

_____
_____

- What things contribute to the dis-ease in your life? Are they external or internal?

What makes maintaining self-control difficult?

_____
_____

- What desires, appetites, and vices threaten your happiness?

No one knows your inner most workings but you.

_____
_____

- My temper robs me of my happiness when ...

Anger is such a strong emotions, what causes it for you?

_____
_____

Empathy

- Is there a group, program, or service you've always wanted to develop at your job or offer in your business?
Exercising your ability to provide a solution for others is amazing. We are all capable of creating impact.

_____

_____

- Who can I mentor, guide, or assist on their journey.
Recognize that you are gifted, and have so much to give. Who can you help step into their greatness.

_____

_____

- Where or who can I show more tolerance?
Sometimes people need room, time, and space to grow. You have to know when to give feedback and when to hold back.

_____

_____

- What situations, socially or globally, can I be more understanding of?
There's so much going on in our world that affects us and the people we're around every day. Try to be more socially aware and understand what people are going through around you. This will help you identify and relate to more people, on a deeper level.

_____

_____

Building Relationships

- I am still upset with "(name)" because…

Are you still holding on to "something" with "someone?" Where can you let something go to achieve more peace and happiness? Remember forgiveness is for you.

_____
_____

- If I minimized and/or eliminated my interaction with "(name)" certain situations would be less stressful.

When boundaries aren't enough, you have to know when to let go.

_____
_____

- Do you need to create a new social/professional circle?

It's okay to have more than one circle. Don't be afraid to develop new relationships. Remember, you are the sum of the five people you interact with most.

_____
_____

- Where do I need more balance in my relationships? Where can I create more depth?

Are you receiving the emotional support, spiritual support, love, and encouragement you need from the people in your current circle? Are most of your relationships superficial?

_____
_____

Chapter 6
EQ and your Career

Multiple studies by some of the top companies in the world have shown that when time and energy goes into developing emotional intelligence amongst staff members, productivity levels rise. For years we have placed a high emphasis on IQ, but today, EQ is becoming increasingly more important. We are living in a time like no other. Having emotional intelligence is no longer an option, it's a requirement for success and elevation in the world we live in today.

This is the first time in history that we're looking at a workforce that is made of five completely different generations of people. We have the "traditionalists" (pre-1946), these are generally our mentors, people who are known to be wise, and those whom we seek counsel from. They traditionally believe in hard work, experience, and stability. Then we have the "baby boomers" (1946-1964), who are known for having strong work ethic, associating respect with tenure, and frequently sacrificing their life and family time for a career and status. Next we have "gen-x" (1965-1976), this was the first generation to really challenge the workforce. This generation began to focus more on themselves, looking for opportunities to be recognized individually for performance. They began to challenge the structural hierarchy, of time vs. performance, they wanted companies to be more involved and become a part of what makes them get. They yearned for development, training, rewards, and individual recognition. Next, we have the "millennials," born from (1977-1997). This generation shifted the workforce in a major way. For one people of this generation don't find themselves recognizing loyalty or staying at a company for twenty, thirty years. They are often looking for the best opportunity overall. They are not enthused by titles or stature, they respect performance. Millennials seek to find a place to work that provides professional and personal development. They're more in tuned with finding a place where they can achieve a healthy sense of work/life balance. Because they were introduced to technology at such a young age they aren't afraid of change and how quickly it evolves, unlike the previous generations. Last, but not least, we have "gen z," those who were born after 1997. Although it's still early and there's not a ton of research on this generation, we are seeing a rise in dissertations and studies on this generation as we come along. This generation was born with technology in their hands, a part of their daily lives, and it makes up a great deal of their day. They were the first generation to be exposed to social media in the way that it is presented today. Due to this high connection to digital communication, social media is often the center focus of how they communicate.

They generally prefer this way over a face-to-face interaction. In addition, gen z has witnessed and experienced a level of fear, threat, and anxiety that past generations haven't. They are faced with pressure, comparison, and bullying through social media like never before—they've experienced even worse when it comes to their safety especially in schools. Gen z has seen and experienced foreign and domestic terrorism, violence, and social warfare in a way that's never been displayed before. They have access to news, videos, and photographs twenty-four-seven. This has added an extreme amount of emotion and sensitivity to this generation. With that said, gen z often seeks guidance, structure, and wants to feel safe in their work place. They want to know that their workplace cares about them and their social views as well. Gen z looks for predictability in a work place environment.

Now, along with having five generations in the workforce, we also have a more diverse group of people working together amongst teams today. Although we have a long way to go, thanks to the dedication and sacrifices of those who came before us, the workforce looks extremely different today than it did years ago. Although there's still a lot of work to be done, we are looking at an era where the acknowledgment of diversity is at an all time high. Which is a great thing—but when I say diversity I'm not just talking about having more people of color on our teams or in leadership positions. We are in a place where companies and major corporations are developing ERG's (employee resources groups) outside of ethnicity. New ERG's are being developed for people with disabilities, the LGBTQI community, single parents that work, military families, people effected by trauma and various others. People are finally able to come to work as themselves, open, honest, and getting the support and resources they need from the companies they're dedicating their lives to.

Even though some companies have established these groups, it doesn't mean that everyone automatically supports and/or understands the need for them. This may often lead to misconduct and/or miscommunication amongst staff members. In addition, there are a lot of companies that haven't established any ERG's yet. Mostly because they don't recognize the need for them or they don't have the staff, time, funding, or structure to implement them effectively. So what do we end up with? Different people, from different backgrounds, of different ethnicities, that have different cultural views, who live different lifestyles, all trying to come together for the same purpose. This alone, requires an extreme amount of emotional intelligence.

EQ isn't only important for things like bridging the generation gap or creating diverse teams— it also significantly impacts a company's cultural and moral. Think about it, are you at a company that has a good culture and moral? In what ways do you contribute to this atmosphere? Does leadership reflect the ideals that the company is founded on? Does your company even define what that is or what it looks like? When you display a strong sense of emotional intelligence you will stand out from the crowd. People will be drawn to you, they will trust you, and feel comfortable with relying on you in times of difficulty and stress. We aren't robots, we have to interact with people on a daily basis—and that interaction is what creates a company's atmosphere.

I placed EQ in your career after self, love, and happiness, because you have to be fulfilled from a holistic place before you can contribute to others in a way that is powerful and positive. Your level of emotional intelligence will determine how far you'll go in your career, and how fast you'll get there. Even as an entrepreneur these same tools and techniques apply. Things like managing your emotions, knowing your strengths and weaknesses, your commitment level, adaptability, resilience, social skills, your aura, and your ability to self-motivate matter when it comes to success.

People who develop a strong sense of emotional intelligence excel in ways that are evident to others. They have a strong sense of character and generally have a huge impact on associates, clients, and other staff members. People with a high EQ are trusted with special projects, achieve higher visibility due to reliability, they excel in leadership roles, and they are easier, more pleasant to work with. No matter what business you're in, it's the people business—and it pays for people to know, like, and trust you. You make more sales when people genuinely like you, when it comes time for reviews and promotions you're seen in a better light; and when you interact with your team in a positive way you inspire them to be better, creating impact and showing leadership.

As we move on to explore the ways you can apply and enhance your emotional intelligence in your career and/or business, I want you think about your "why?" Why have you chosen the career you're in? Was it a choice, or did you just fall into it? Are you passionate about what you do? People often forget that their career/job/business is a huge part of their lives. On average we spend more time working and engaging with our co-workers/business partners, than we do with our family's, caring for our loved ones, taking part in leisure activities, and/or restoring ourselves.

So it's imperative that you are enjoying, excelling, and creating impact within your field. You need to know what you want, how you plan to get there, who you'll need to help you, and how to be effective in doing so. Building your emotional intelligence will help you acquire this knowledge base. It will also boost your confidence, push you to be great in your field, position you to achieve greater levels of success, and help you maintain a healthy balanced life overall. So, let's get to it!

Applying EQ to Your Career
Self-Awareness

- Do you enjoy what you do? Are you passionate about your line of work? Does it fulfill you?

This is one of the most important questions. If you're <u>not</u> happy, what industry would make you feel more fulfilled?

_____
_____

- My plan is to...

Do you know what you want, and how you plan to get to the next level?

_____
_____

- Have you been doing well strategizing on your own?

Develop a personal board of advisors, people close to you, whom you can bounce ideas off of.

_____
_____

- What emotions do you have about the future? Do you bring value to your industry? Are you an innovator?

What are you bringing to the industry?

_____
_____

- What are your strength and growth areas?

You have to know this in order to map out a successful career path.

_____
_____

Self-Control

- Are you mindful of work interactions, do you re-read emails before sending them?

Effective and kind communication is necessary for clarity. It also helps minimize friction amongst associates.

_____
_____

- I dislike "(name)" because he/she _____

Can you set aside personal disputes to work alongside someone you may not like?

_____
_____

- Who or what is dictating my career?

Are you in control or is someone else in control of your decision making when it comes to your career and the choices your make?

_____
_____

- I sometimes speak out of turn when...

Learn to respect others people's time, thoughts, and opinions. Show the respect you desire.

_____
_____

- I can be inflexible when it comes to...

When new policies/procedure arise, learn to adapt quickly.

_____
_____

Empathy

- Who are you most impatient with at work/in business?
Do you bring a personal bias with you?

_____
_____

- What do you have in common with this person?
Stop looking at what you don't like/understand about a person and begin to explore where you can relate.

_____
_____

- Have you thought about things from their perspective?
Different thought processes in a work place, on a team, and within business create the opportunity for new, fresh ideas; embrace it.

_____
_____

- Where do your morals/values lie?
Are you treating people you work with in a way that compliments those morals and values?

_____
_____

- Do you display leadership capabilities? Do you motivate and inspire others to be their best?
Be the shining light, show respect, and you will thrive.

_____
_____

Building Relationships

- Who can you learn from at your company? Who can help you elevate and map out your career?

Seek out these people. Be proactive and strategic when it comes to your mentors and sponsors.

_____

_____

- What do you know about the person who can help you?

Do your research, make sure you connect with the right person; the person that matches your needs and skill sets.

_____

_____

- Is your heart in the right place?

Be genuine when developing professional relationship.

_____

_____

- What do you have to give or offer?

We want our relationships to be mutually beneficial. Find a way to contribute, resolve an issue, or make their life easier, it's a surefire way to build a bond and show your talent.

_____

_____

- What exactly do you want from the relationship?

You have to go in knowing what your agenda is. Are you looking for wisdom, advice, time, mentorship, results, etc.

_____

_____

Enhancing EQ in Your Career
Self-Awareness

- Are you enthusiastic about your job/business? Do you show it?

Don't be afraid to take on a new passion project, something to get you excited and recommitted to the field.

_____
_____

- Who are your key sponsors?

There's a difference between a mentor and a sponsor.

_____
_____

- What tools/techniques do you use for accountability?

Invest in a business/life coach, someone who can take the journey with you, encourage you, and help guide you.

_____
_____

- What are you currently doing to be more mindful?

When you become more present you don't fret over the past and you don't worry about the future.

_____
_____

- Are you willing, or have you thought about a lateral move within your company?

Play to your skill set, but show people you're not afraid of a growth challenge.

_____
_____

Self-Control

- Do you have the capacity to redirect thoughts and actions?

Again, is it kind, is it true, and is it necessary? Practice the art of redirecting negative energy, thoughts, and actions.

_____
_____

- Do you hold on to bad vibes from deals gone wrong, or grudges with people who've done you wrong?

Letting go is for your own peace, sanity, and ability to function properly on a daily basis. Grudges are a result of you allowing the past to live in your present.

_____
_____

- When I have a bad morning, the rest of my day is...

A bad morning, phone call, or email doesn't mean your entire day has to be ruined. Remember your "bounce back routine" at work and in business.

_____
_____

- I resist change when…

Resisting change is about fear, new responsibility, and being uncomfortable. Don't run or resist, adapt and adjust.

_____
_____

Empathy

- Who can you open up a new conversation with to better understand them?

Someone has to take the step to break down the wall. Let it be you.

_____
_____

- How can you get past the surface and superficial?

You can do your job and go home; never relating to or understanding the people you work with. Or you can learn, grow, and collaborate with them on a deeper level.

_____
_____

- Do you encourage people… or patronize them? How?

There's a big difference between being genuinely helpful and being unaware and offensive.

_____
_____

- What morals and values do I need to develop?

Be honest with yourself about opportunities for growth when it comes to your morals, values, and how you treat people. Don't ignore an opportunity to become a better person and create impact.

_____
_____

If you're already amazing, that's wonderful! Maybe you could offer some of your time, help someone else succeed on your team that may be struggling.

Building Relationships

- When was the last time you asked for a meeting?
Don't be intimidated by "higher-ups," be bold and confident. Send the email, make the request, go talk to them, share your ideas, thoughts, and talents!

_____
_____

- Are you prepared for your next opportunity?
When developing next level relationships it's important to perform and exceed expectations.

_____
_____

- Do you need additional training? Do you need more experience? If so, are you prepared to get it?
Know what you need to excel at the next level.

_____
_____

- When was the last time you stepped up?
Raise your hand, take control and/or diffuse situations without having to be told, be a leader, show reliability.

_____
_____

- When I'm around certain people I act like…
Be you. Excel from your level of greatness. Don't get lost in trying to be someone else, people can see it.

_____
_____

Chapter 7
EQ and Conflict

No matter who you are, what you do, what your background is, or how much money you have— at some point in your life you will be faced with conflict, opposing views, and/or confrontation. How we handled those conflicts and disappointments in life, in love, in our career determines our level of happiness. Having resilience isn't always innate. Sometimes it has to be developed. How we process negativity and the way we handle difficulties has a huge impact on our success.

Conflict is neither good nor bad. When we break it down, conflict is just two opposing views amongst particular parties; which is fine. Everyone is entitled to their own views and opinions on certain things. Conflict can also be a when a person experiences an inconvenience when it comes to their needs. Either way, conflict, if not handled properly, can end in self destruction, outlandish behavior, broken relationships, physical altercations, or worse. Fact is, you'll probably deal with conflict in almost every area of our life at some point or another, if you haven't already. So you might as well learn how to deal with it in a way that is productive and not detrimental.

Being able to recognize, assess, understand and mange conflict is key. Let's look at some ways to apply and enhance your emotional intelligence in order to deal with conflict in your life.

Applying EQ to Conflict
Self-Awareness

- Where do you see the most conflict in your life?
First step to dealing with conflict is recognition.

_____
_____

- When was the last time you escalated a conflict?
Awareness is the key to understanding and prevention.

_____
_____

- How does it feel when you're experiencing conflict?
Assess the emotions and feeling behind the conflict so you can better identify and manage them.

_____
_____

- Why are you experiencing such heavy/constant conflict?
Getting to the root of conflict, gives clarity to the solution.

_____
_____

- How can you prevent high level conflict?
Know yourself and the person and/or situation you're dealing with. Generally we can see conflict way before emotions begin to flare.

_____
_____

Self-Control

- Some of my triggers are….

Know and understand your triggers, what sets you off.

_____
_____

- I need to step away when...

It's okay to remove yourself from a situation when tensions are high.

_____
_____

- I hit below the belt when...

Words and actions can't be undone. Refrain from trying to hurt someone during conflict.

_____
_____

- I create conflict when change occurs because...

Sometimes people create conflict as a result of uncertainty or fear, they need time to process. Identify the emotion and categorize it appropriately.

_____
_____

- How strong is your faith? How can you make it stronger?

Whatever conflict you're facing in life, it's temporary; and you have the power to change it.

_____
_____

Empathy

- When was the last time you compromised?
Learn how to work with people, not against them

_____

_____

- What does your body language say during conflict?
Showing apathy or aggression can escalate a difference of opinion. Attentiveness, understanding, and a calm demeanor may help.

_____

_____

- Do you show respect for the other party during conflict?
Be mindful of the way you approach the topic matter. You may have more experience, or know more about a particular topic, but don't be dismissive or condescending.

_____

_____

- Are you willing to learn from someone else?
Be ever learning, even in conflict there's always something to learn from the situation or the other person.

_____

_____

- Do you read people well? Can you sense their emotions?
Sometimes pain is the only way (some) people know how to communicate— due to past experiences and/or trauma.

_____

_____

Building Relationships

- Are you aware of how you engage during conflict?
No relationship is identical. Your response to conflict with your boss, spouse, child, or friend will all be different.

___
___

- Do you monitor personal space during conflict?
Maintain a safe and neutral distance during conflict.

___
___

- Do you listen to your gut during conflict?
If you feel like a conversation or situation is about to take a turn for the worse, listen to your spirit!

___
___

- Do you have access to a neutral party?
Sometimes having a third party takes the pressure off a situation. It allows both parties to feel freedom and/or comfort during the disagreement.

___
___

- Where is your self-esteem?
Stand up for yourself. You set the bar for how people talk to you and/or treat you during conflict. It's okay to disagree, but disrespect should never be tolerated.

___
___

Enhancing EQ within Conflict
Self-Awareness

- How can you implement change when it comes to conflict in your life?
Where can you alter your approach to certain situations?

_____
_____

- Have you communicated your thoughts effectively?
Often time's conflict occurs because there's a simple miscommunication.

_____
_____

- Have you taken the proper steps towards a resolution?
Don't leave negative feelings/emotions in the air. Communicate, listen, and come to a resolution.

_____
_____

- Are you an active listener? Do you listen to respond?
Be open to hearing what the person has to say. Ask open ended questions that allow the person to get their true feelings across.

_____
_____

- What are you good at during conflict?
Do you remain calm, breath deep, count to ten, walk away, etc.? Use the techniques that you're good at.

_____
_____

Self-Control

- People bring me out of character when...

Don't allow other people, who thrive on conflict, to draw you in— don't give them that power.

_____
_____

- I am able to maintain my composure when...

Highlight the moments when you succeed. Recognize what allowed you to remain calm.

_____
_____

- I can be accommodating when...

When stakes are high, relationships are at risk, or careers are on line, you have to know when to give in and be accommodating. Sometimes the conflict isn't worth the damage.

_____
_____

- Do you need to take a second look in the mirror?

Sometimes the other person does have more experience, education, knowledge, and/or expertise. Know when to respect and honor wisdom with respect.

_____
_____

Empathy

- Are you able to lead by example during a conflict?

When we shift our energy, most often the other person will shift their energy to match yours.

_____

_____

- Do you often shut people down in conflict?

Be mindful of presenting demands and ultimatums during a conflict. This energy can become extremely hostile.

_____

_____

- I can be dismissive when...

Ask questions to help show the person you understand.

_____

_____

- Do you use jokes or a playful attitude to pacify a situation?

A joke or playful smile can either alleviate the tension or elevate the conflict. Know your counterpart before executing a light joke to relieve tension.

_____

_____

- I leave most conflicts feeling...

You shouldn't feel defeated after a disagreement. Take time to debrief, decompress, and release any unwanted energy.

_____

_____

Building Relationships

- Can you admit when you're wrong? Will you apologize?
A lot can happen during conflict, an apology can go a long way.

- Do you need to explore therapy (with family member, friend, or spouse) or have an HR mediator (with a co-worker) to help resolve any deep rooted conflict?
Any time there is constant conflict to the point of dysfunction, sometimes professional help is warranted.

- Do you have to continue this relationship?
When you're dealing with co-workers, family, or your spouse be open to growing <u>with</u> them. These are high frequency people in your life, people who aren't going away any time soon. So try to make it work.

- Is this relationship toxic? Does it need to be mended?
Your thoughts, idea, and opinions are real and deserve respect. If you find yourself constantly in conflict with one person in particular, maybe you need to reevaluate the relationship.

I hope these questions brought you some new clarity and placed you in a position to gain a new perspective as to where you are and what you can do. We are all incredible beings, capable of achieving anything we put our hearts and minds to. However, it's essential that we understand the importance of taking the time to examine ourselves and our lives from an introspective place. Turning inward is always the answer to achieving outward success.

Know yourself, control your emotions, be understanding, and build strong relationships! So go, and step into your greatness.

www.ingramcontent.com/pod-product-compliance
Lightning Source LLC
Chambersburg PA
CBHW050020230526
45470CB00003B/1063